Stop Being Mediocre

100 Ways To Become Wealthier, Healthier, and Successful

By

Raza Hussain MD

INFINITY PUBLISHING

ISBN 978-0-7414-6514-6
Library of Congress Control Number: 2011923403

Printed in the United States of America

Published April 2021

INFINITY PUBLISHING
1094 New DeHaven Street, Suite 100
West Conshohocken, PA 19428-2713
Toll-free (877) BUY BOOK
Local Phone (610) 941-9999
Fax (610) 941-9959
Info@buybooksontheweb.com
www.buybooksontheweb.com

Stop Being Mediocre

Acknowledgements

I'd like to thank my family, friends, and anyone who has helped to make me a better person.

Introduction

Who am I and why did I write this book? I'm a resident family physician in my last few months of training before I become an attending physician. I grew up in central Arkansas in a place called Pine Bluff. I had a normal childhood and my parents tried to instill discipline in me at an early age. My father was a family physician by trade as well. I wrote this book because most people are settling in life. They are settling with their work, their bad habits, their choice of life partner, their home, and the list goes on. I feel that people don't live up to their full potential. People give up on themselves and their dreams way too early. I wrote this book as a quick read that can be picked up over and over again. If you apply the principles in this book, you will see changes in your life. I am not an attorney, a CPA, or a relationship counselor. I'm a physician. I know what hard work, dedication, and discipline are. I have also made lots of mistakes in life; I am not perfect by any means. I try to get better every day, and I think anyone can get better if he or she decides to. It's never too late to make a change in your life. I did not use statistics in this book. These ideas have been gathered from my own reading and life experiences. Stop being mediocre and live life to the fullest.

-1-

READ READ READ!!! Go get a library card. The books are FREE. It doesn't get much easier than that. You can also go to a bookstore and buy a book instead of buying something useless. Read about history, politics, finance, self-improvement, or a hundred other things. Just do it and stop being like MOST people…clueless.

-2-

Take RESPONSIBILITY. That means take responsibility for your actions. Your appearance. Your job performance. Your relationships. Your finances. Your weight. Your health. Your present. Your future.

-3-

Quit smoking TODAY...It takes the average person 5 to 7 times to quit smoking. Do it now! Smoking 1 to 3 packs a day is a $5 to $15 a day habit. That money could be invested in an IRA. Smoking doesn't just cause lung cancer...it affects you from head to toe. It can cause bladder cancer, coronary disease, kidney cancer, and a myriad of other health complications. Do yourself and your loved ones a favor...QUIT!

-4-

Be HUMBLE. Humility goes a long way. Whether you're a physician, a corporate attorney, a CEO, a multimillionaire entrepreneur, or a janitor, be humble and down to earth. The opposite of humble is arrogant. Arrogance stems from insecurity…remember, there's always someone smarter, better looking, and more successful.

-5-

Go back to school. If you didn't graduate from high school, get your GED. Do you want a bachelor's degree in chemistry or history? Go get one. Did you always want your master's in psychology but never found the time? Today is the day to make time. Go get a law degree. Go to medical school. Go to culinary school. Lose the excuses! Education is invaluable.

-6-

Have a yearly physical examination. Call your primary care provider today. Don't have one? Get one. Just like if you never get your car serviced and wonder why it falls apart. The human body is the same way. Ten years without a visit to the doctor…just plain stupid. Years of uncontrolled hypertension, diabetes, high cholesterol, etc. can lead to an early grave. It's preventable. Don't be stupid. Take control of your health.

-7-

Lose resentments. This harbored anger leads to underlying stress that can be manifested by real somatic or physical ailments. Forgive your exes; forgive your current spouse, boyfriend, or girlfriend; forgive your parents, your teachers, yourself, your friends, your dog, your parole officer, your mailman, etc. Life is short. Move forward, not backward.

-8-

Leave your legacy. How do you want to be remembered? Leave your mark on this world before you go. I don't mean rob a bank either. One way is by writing a book. People years from now will be able to pick up your book and read it long after you're gone. There are lots of other ways. Don't be mediocre and lazy, like most people. Chip away at it daily.

-9-

Quit drinking today! It's the biggest waste of time, money, and productivity. It's the only drug that can kill you from withdrawal from it. Not heroin, cocaine, or methamphetamine…but your good ole buddy alcohol. The average person that consumes alcohol regularly may spend upwards of $100,000 on its consumption over the course of a lifetime. What a waste! You'd be better off buying a Porsche. At least you'd have something tangible to show for it. The only ones that gain anything are the ones selling it. Also, alcohol affects every organ system in the body. It can elevate blood pressure, kill your liver, give you memory problems, give you erectile dysfunction, ruin your pancreas, and the list goes on.

-10-

Take a vacation…the grind can wait. Whether it's Rome, Georgia, or Rome, Italy, take a break. Take that trip. Recharge your batteries. Forget about everything going on in your life that may be causing you stress. Take a breather from the monotony and enjoy life. You never know, you may not be here next year or next month. Never take life for granted.

-11-

Strive to be the BEST in your profession. If your goal is simply to get by, then you're in the WRONG line of work. If you look at your watch every five minutes to see if you're five minutes closer to being done for the day, then it's time to reevaluate your situation. There needs to be some element of passion in what you're doing.

-12-

If you want to be SUCCESSFUL, study SUCCESS and SUCCESSFUL people. You don't have to reinvent the wheel. Yes, it's that simple.

-13-

Get rid of EVERY toxic or negative person in your life. I don't care if you've known them for 20 years. If the toxic people in your life are family, then keep a healthy distance. Toxic people will not let you succeed and want to keep you mediocre, like them.

-14-

Reflect daily. Reflect on your day, your week, your life. Take time to enjoy your growth and your accomplishments. Also, take time to reflect on your mistakes. This daily introspection is a MUST to move forward.

-15-

Be COMPLIANT with your medications. The instructions are written out for you. If you're not sure how to take your medications, ask your physician. If you're diabetic and taking 20 units of insulin every day, then do that. Tight control of your medical problems today can prevent horrible outcomes in the future.

-16-

Meet with a Certified Financial Planner (CFP). It doesn't matter if you make $30,000 per year or $300,000 per year. A financial planner will help you create a game plan for where you want to go. Most Americans have nothing in the bank. Ask around and find a reputable CFP. Stop being mediocre and take action today.

-17-

Be DISCIPLINED. That means wake up 30 minutes early to read or to exercise. Or turn off the TV so you can write your next book. Most people take the path of least resistance. That's why most people end up with below-average results.

-18-

STOP blaming others for your problems. Blame yourself. Once you've accepted responsibility then you can take action. If you're overweight, broke, uneducated, or an endless list of other things, decide right now that you're going to do something about it.

-19-

Stop going to the ER for every little thing. If you've been shot, broke your leg, were in a car wreck, had a heart attack, etc., I understand. If you have minor things going on, such as itchy feet—yes, I have seen this in the ER—or the sniffles, a sore throat, a cough, make an appointment with your primary care provider. You can also go to an urgent care/walk-in clinic. That's what these facilities are designed for. ER visits are going up annually. There's a reason ER physicians have one of the highest burnout/attrition rates in all of medicine...people not using common sense. Don't be one of these people, please!

-20-

STOP eating fast food. The only thing fast about it is the speed in which it enlarges your ass. Once in a blue moon, or even once a month is okay, but c'mon, people. You can't eat this stuff weekly or like a lot of people…daily.

-21-

Start exercising TODAY! You don't have to have a $60-a-month gym membership. You can start walking every day at least 30 minutes to an hour. You can jog daily or at least three to four times a week. You can go swimming, biking, or whatever else helps you burn calories. Exercise has tons of benefits…it promotes better sleep, it's fun, it boosts your energy level, it improves psychological well-being, it helps to reduce or maintain body weight, and the list goes on.

-22-

Be confident. Confidence is sexy; people are attracted to it, and are willing to listen to you when you have it. Always look people in the eyes when speaking. Everyone has a unique swagger and style. Confident people are better at being decisive. Act as if….you own the place, you have no worries, etc. Keep a healthy balance…don't tread into the arrogance domain.

-23-

Tell your loved ones and the people you care about that you love them and care about them. My father passed away unexpectedly in March 2008, and I would give anything to tell him one more time that I love him. Do this today.

-24-

Be positive. ALWAYS think positive. You can accomplish more if you're always positive instead of negative. Replace negative thoughts with positive ones. Your thoughts are in YOUR control.

-25-

Start your own business. Stop making someone else rich. There are so many benefits from tax breaks to controlling your own destiny. Do some planning, then go for it. Take action! Start a business in whatever you're passionate about.

-26-

True growth comes from painful experiences. When you don't personally experience some kind of difficult situation from a mistake, it is difficult to learn from it. If you can learn from others' mistakes, that would be ideal, but most people will repeat the same mistakes if there are no REAL consequences.

-27-

STOP pushing your kids into careers they do not want to do or are not suited for. If your family has three generations of doctors, accountants, attorneys, etc., that's wonderful, but if your kid is talented in sports and wants to pursue that, then try to nurture that talent. If your son or daughter becomes an attorney just to get your approval, he or she will be mediocre and unsatisfied. In a matter of time, they will probably do something else that brings them personal fulfillment and success.

-28-

Remember…ONE great idea that you generate and act upon can be the difference between greatness and mediocrity.

-29-

Lose weight! Obesity is not attractive and it's not healthy. It causes unnecessary health problems from osteoarthritis due to extra weight on the knees, hips, and ankles. It can cause high cholesterol, high blood pressure, diabetes, low self-esteem, and depression, to name a few. Take responsibility for yourself now and improve the quality of your life.

-30-

NEVER share your new ideas with other people. People get jealous and they get insecure. That includes friends and even family members. If you want to start a new business, go back to school, or whatever…be careful about whom you tell because they will try to keep you at their level…mediocre. Focus on your goal, bring it to fruition, and no one will be able to stop you.

-31-

STOP procrastinating. You know what you have to do. That thing you've been putting off for weeks or months…do it NOW!

-32-

Have a HEALTHY SEX life. So that means being married and having sex once a year on your birthday is not a healthy sex life. Sex burns calories, relieves stress, builds self-esteem, improves intimacy…the list goes on.

-33-

Go get your passport made. If you've never left the country, this one step is necessary and will get the ball rolling. This goes back to stepping out of your comfort zone. It will be easier for you to envision going thousands of miles from home base once you have that passport.

-34-

Contribute to your 401(k)! A lot of employers will match you up to a certain amount. That's free money. A retirement savings plan of some sort is a good idea if you would like to retire someday. Most Americans have no savings. Please DON'T be one of these people.

-35-

Learn a NEW language. Speaking "American" does not count. Learning a new language can increase job opportunities, open the door to new cultures, and can intellectually stimulate you. So challenge yourself—Spanish, French, Urdu, German, Marshallese? You pick. There are roughly six to seven thousand languages out there, so you have plenty to pick from!

-36-

Choose your friends WISELY. You may not know it, but your friends could be keeping you down. There's a saying that when you hang out with trash you start to smell like it. Your friends usually determine where you set the bar for yourself. The more successful your friends are, the higher you usually set the bar for yourself.

-37-

TALK to your kids about sex. I have treated lots of clueless teens who have no idea what they're doing. They have no idea about contraception or sexually transmitted diseases (STDs). It's your responsibility as a parent to provide some foundation on this subject.

-38-

Turn your car into a place to LEARN. Turn off the radio. The same songs are played over and over and over. You're not missing anything. Go to the library and check out some books on CD, or go buy some books on CD and start your own collection.

-39-

Please stop giving your kids STUPID names. You're already placing them at a disadvantage before they can even walk. If a name is usually spelled with one A, then adding 3 more in a row for effect is not smart. Leave your creative endeavors to other outlets. You'll thank me one day.

-40-

Please use protection. I don't mean carry a gun. I mean please wear condoms. Yes, some things can be treated with antibiotics such as chlamydia and gonorrhea. That doesn't mean it's okay to go around playing Russian roulette with your privates. Some STDs are for life…like herpes…that's the gift that keeps on giving.

-41-

Volunteer your time. Teach someone how to read. Contact your local literacy council. Go serve food at your local homeless shelter. You CAN spare an hour a week.

-42-

Discipline your kids. I have had kids of all ages speak disrespectfully to me in the hospital while their parents sit there and think it's okay. If I did that, my mother would have taken me to the car and pimp-slapped me! I don't mean punch your kid in the face as if you're in a prizefight, but do let them know that it is not okay. Manners and respect are vital to have a successful future. Your kids aren't made of porcelain. It's okay to let them know what's right and wrong. Don't be a mediocre parent and don't let your kids become mediocre adults.

-43-

SAVE at least 10% of your monthly income. If you're a real badass, try to save 15% or 20%. Invested properly, those savings can turn into some SERIOUS cash over time with compound interest.

-44-

STOP living above your means. If you make $50,000 a year, you should be living like someone who makes $40,000 a year, not someone who earns $100,000 a year. Stop being mediocre…no one cares that you're driving a car that you CAN'T afford.

-45-

Tell your parents, "Thank you." Tell whoever got you where you are today, "THANKS." No one is successful all by him- or herself.

-46-

STOP eating when you get full. That's a simple concept, but most Americans don't follow it. If you're at a restaurant and you've eaten half of what's on your plate—stop. If you're full and there's plenty left on your plate—take it home. There's no law that says you have to finish EVERYthing on your plate.

-47-

Take the word CAN'T out of your vocabulary. That word is for mediocre people.

-48-

Be a mentor. You have some type of life experience or work experience that would greatly benefit someone. Whether you're a plumber or a neurosurgeon, you can help someone on his or her journey to become a huge success.

-49-

Have a library in your home. Whether it's large or small, you NEED one. Once you start adding to it and reading, it will become a good positive addiction. Don't be mediocre like most people and not have touched a book in years.

-50-

Try a NEW restaurant. STOP eating at the same damn restaurant. Eating somewhere new won't kill you. Broaden your horizons. Better yet, try an entirely different type of cuisine. Never had sushi? Well, then today is the day to try sushi.

-51-

When YOU make a mistake, admit it, correct it, and move forward. Don't dwell on mistakes, no matter how large you may think they are.

-52-

FAILURE is a part of SUCCESS. Don't be scared to try things because you're scared to fail. That's all part of the process. The more times you fail, the better your chances of success. Only mediocre people don't try because they're scared of what others may think or say about them if they fail.

-53-

STOP relying on medications for EVERY little thing. Sometimes you can have a bad day…that's LIFE. You don't need an antidepressant if you've had a couple of bad days. Try to work things out for yourself. Use medications as a last resort.

-54-

Practice DELAYED gratification. If you DON'T have the money to buy something, then DON'T buy whatever it is that is tempting you. Whatever you buy will likely lose its value but you will still be PAYING for it.

-55-

NEVER gossip about people behind their backs. It shows a LACK of integrity and shows people you have a character flaw. If you do talk about someone, say something positive or don't say anything at all.

-56-

Happiness is a CHOICE. You can choose to be happy or you can choose to be bitter and pissed off. I suggest going the happiness route. Life is short—why not BE HAPPY!

-57-

NEVER have only one way to earn money. If that one source of income is gone due to being fired, downsizing, injury, etc., you become a drain on society. There are countless ways to earn additional income. Figure out what works for you.

-58-

Make sure you LEARN something new every day. A new word, a new skill, a new anything!

-59-

Get a pet. Pets such as cats and dogs can lower stress levels. Pets love you unconditionally and can elevate your mood. I don't recommend any pets that can kill you or raise your stress level. If a tiger running around your house or apartment is your idea of a good time, then more power to you!

-60-

WRITE your goals down. By writing your goals down, it makes them more real to your subconscious. First, you need to have goals, so take some time and figure out what you want. Once you have them written down, ACT on them.

-61-

STOP living your life according to how others want you to live it. If your family wanted you to become an accountant but you wanted to become an architect, you will NEVER be happy. DON'T worry about what others think—do what makes YOU happy.

-62-

Get a higher power into your life. If you've fallen off the spiritual wagon, it's time to get back on. It doesn't matter what name you call it as long as you use it to propel you forward. Never underestimate faith and how it can make you successful!

-63-

If you aren't happy with where you are in life, the only person responsible is YOU. The beauty of this situation is YOU can fix it right now. You can STOP doing the things that make you unhappy or unsuccessful.

-64-

Sign a prenuptial agreement! This is not the most romantic concept out there, but you will thank me if things go south. Roughly HALF of all marriages in this country end in divorce. Be smart and be prepared. If your marriage is meant to work out, IT WILL. A prenup is not going to be the reason your marriage will or won't work.

-65-

Keep a journal of your thoughts, experiences, dreams, favorite quotes, and whatever else is of value to you. The value of the content in your journal will be priceless. Try to write in your journal daily.

-66-

Whatever the majority of people are doing with their lives…do the OPPOSITE! Creativity, innovation, and wealth do NOT go hand in hand with following the masses.

-67-

Don't be another person who tries a new fad diet and fails. Diets only work when you follow the diet. When you STOP the diet, the weight usually RETURNS. If you want to lose weight, you need to be disciplined. Losing weight is a lifestyle choice. You need to EXERCISE and eat BETTER. There's no getting around it!

-68-

NEVER drink and drive! I can't stress this enough. I don't care if you have had two beers and feel fine. Every state has laws on what is considered the legal limit. It's NOT worth the risk. The implications it can have on your life, career, family, wallet, etc. are not worth it. You may injure or, worse, KILL someone or yourself. ALWAYS take a cab or let a designated driver take the wheel if you decide to drink.

-69-

Be SELFISH with your TIME! Stop saying yes to every person that asks you for your time. Time is the only thing that there is a finite amount of for each person. Time is very precious! When you WASTE it, it's GONE forever. A homeless person and a billionaire have the same 24 hours in a day…what are YOU doing with YOUR time?!

-70-

Mediocrity is contagious! If you hang around ignorant, mediocre people who have low standards, chances are, you are exactly the SAME as them. The solution is to STOP hanging around those people and get NEW friends.

-71-

On your road to wealth and success, there are two things you NEVER want to skimp on…your attorney and your CPA. They will be two crucial components of your team and you want to find the absolute BEST!

-72-

Where you are in life is a direct result of YOUR thoughts. Change your thoughts and you can change your life. Think about misery and lack all day…guess what…that's why your life isn't what you want it to be. Think POSITIVE thoughts daily! Think about where you want to go in life, NOT what you don't want in life.

-73-

If you have a few very close friends that you can share your thoughts and time with, you are better off than most people are. Having a collection of acquaintances means nothing. I guarantee if you call one of these "friends" at three in the morning with an emergency they won't help you. You should be a close friend in return to those same few people.

-74-

When you talk about your problems constantly to other people they secretly find pleasure in the fact that you HAVE problems. They also want to run when they see you coming! Stop being mediocre! Keep your problems to yourself while you work on the solutions to them.

-75-

Everyone will think about quitting on the road to success. People's natural tendency is to do what's EASY and requires the least amount of effort. Think about throwing in the towel all you want as long as you DON'T actually do it! By continuing and persisting on your journey, you are better off than MOST people.

-76-

Don't try to change people, only change YOURSELF. People change when they are ready and that may be NEVER. People still smoke after they have been diagnosed with cancer. People still drink alcohol after they have cirrhosis of the liver. People do strange things and fear change. So worry about YOURSELF.

-77-

Everyone is SELLING something. You may be selling an idea, a product, or a service. A doctor is selling his knowledge, procedural skill, and medical expertise to a patient. A lawyer is selling his legal skill and expertise to a client. EVERYONE has CUSTOMERS! They are called different things by different people…patients, students, clients, and so on. Make your customers HAPPY, or they can always go somewhere else.

-78-

SMILE every day. Whether you want to or not. Just do it even if you're alone. Do it especially in public and when you greet someone. Smiling has so many benefits…it can change your mood, give you confidence, and make you look younger, just to name a few.

-79-

Go on a date. It doesn't matter if you're single, married, or have a boyfriend/girlfriend. Shake things up a little. Get dressed up, spray on some cologne or perfume, and go out. If you're married and stuck in a routine, then tell your spouse to be ready tonight for a night on the town.

-80-

Go to a museum. Your town, no matter how small, has a museum or one close by. Broaden your horizons. Experience the history of your town, state, country, and world.

-81-

Dream BIG. Do it big or don't do it all. I've heard people say if your dreams don't scare you, you're not dreaming big enough.

-82-

Be GRATEFUL for everything you have. Someone may have it better than you, but millions of people have it WORSE than you.

-83-

Get some SLEEP! More and more people are not getting enough sleep. Sleep has tons of benefits from helping your memory, to controlling your mood, and making you feel like a million bucks, to name a few. Six to eight hours a night should do the trick.

-84-

Have a good LAUGH. Life is not that serious. Go rent a funny movie or go see a stand-up comic…TODAY.

-85-

NEVER envy anyone. You can achieve what someone else has accomplished and then some.

-86-

Make a will. This may seem like a morbid subject, but it's very important unless you want the government taking what you've worked hard for your entire life. Get an attorney—specifically one specializing in estate law—and get it done!

-87-

Set GOALS. There is no goal that is too big to conquer. Visualize your goals. Write your goals down, and then take daily steps to achieve them.

-88-

Walk to work. If you live a mile or two away, don't be lazy and drive. If it's raining or snowing, that's one thing, but save on gas and shed some pounds.

-89-

NEVER open a store credit card. There's NO reason for it. The interest rates are ridiculous. If you have one, pay off the balance and get rid of it.

-90-

Be spontaneous. Life is about having FUN! Do something out of the ordinary today.

-91-

Find a mentor. There is someone out there that can help you become more successful. There are people out there that have already accomplished what you want to in life. Get rid of your pride and ask for help. That person may already be in your life.

-92-

Remove LAZINESS from your life. Lazy people are mediocre. Do not be one of these people.

-93-

STOP buying new cars. Only a small percentage of people can TRULY afford a new car in the first place. A new car loses a substantial amount of its value the minute it is driven off the lot. Let someone else take the financial kick between the legs.

-94-

ALWAYS be punctual! Even showing up a few minutes early won't kill you. Showing up late is not fashionable—it just makes you look like a jackass.

-95-

If someone comes to you excited with a NEW idea, DON'T shoot it down or belittle it. Don't let your own insecurities rain on someone else's parade.

-96-

Keep your political views to YOURSELF. You look ridiculous, intolerant, and ignorant when you rant about politics in public. When you bash a certain politician or political party in front of others, you don't know whom you're offending.

-97-

If you are in a failing relationship, DON'T cheat. Just end the relationship. Leave the relationship with some integrity and try again.

-98-

Most people think that learning stops when they finish school and get a diploma. That kind of thinking is for MEDIOCRE people. You should be learning DAILY. Lifelong learning is a requirement if you want to be successful.

-99-

DON'T text and drive. No text is worth getting into an accident or dying. This one is self-explanatory.

-100-

STOP using dipping tobacco or snuff. It makes you look ridiculous, uneducated, and it is a waste of money. The biggest reason not to…it causes cancer!

Made in the USA
Monee, IL
04 November 2026

67380520R00066